Dear Friends,

Thank you from the bottom of my heart for your overwhelming support of Under the Big Tent: Election Year. Your belief in this story, which celebrates the values that unite us, means so much. It is a privilege to share this journey with you, and I am deeply grateful for your commitment to teaching the next generation about the importance of civic engagement, responsibility, and love of country.

With heartfelt appreciation,
MCJ

Election Year: Under The Big Tent is a whimsical children's story set in a vibrant circus where animals run for election to become the leader. The tale begins with excitement as four candidates—a lion, a monkey, a donkey, and a grand elephant—enter the race, each promising to make the circus a better place. The lion boasts of honor, the monkey offers bananas, and the donkey takes a laid-back approach, while the elephant, known for his wisdom and grace, vows to unite the circus.

The animals debate and perform, vying for votes under the big top, but in the end, it's the grand elephant who wins the election. With the circus united, the story concludes with a message about leadership and the joy of participating in a fair and fun election. Through colorful characters and lively action, the book teaches children about democracy, leadership, and the importance of making thoughtful decisions.

Illustrated by
SANJAY SINGH

&

Formatted by
FARIHA ANDLEEB

In a magical land, where colors were grand, Lived animals quite wise, in a circus so planned. Election time had come, with excitement so bold, The circus was buzzing, tales to be told.

In a circus so grand, with colors so bright, Animals gathered, oh what a sight! Election year had come to the big top, A circus of politics, a show that won't stop!

Four candidates emerged with dreams in their eyes, To win the election, they'd aim (pay) for the skies.

A lion roared loud, with his mighty fine mane, "I'll lead this great circus, bring honor, no shame!" A monkey chimed in, with a grin on his face, "Bananas for all, it's a tasty embrace!"

But a hush fell upon them, as trumpets did sound, The grand elephant entered, a leader renowned. With tusks gleaming bright, and a regal attire, He stepped to the front, setting hearts on fire.

With a trunk for speeches, he'd take a strong stand. Reflecting on business, and the lay of the land!

The grand elephant spoke, with a voice full of grace, "Let's have a fair election, may the best one take place. I promise a circus, where all can partake, Jugglers, acrobats, and even the snake."

In the heart of the tent, a stage was prepared, A podium stood, where debates would be shared. Candidates lined up, with passion ablaze, To win the circus votes, in various ways.

The monkey swung high, with his tricks in the air, The lion roared fiercely, with a wild lion's glare.

"Donkey," said the lion, "it's time to wake, Join the election, for goodness' sake!". The old sleepy donkey, not so spry nor astute, Entered the stage, in his old worn-out suit.

The donkey yawned, with a twinkle in his eye, "Let's not rush decisions, just relax, oh my! I'll join the race but take it slow, for this is as fast, as fast that I go."

The debate was a spectacle, under the big top, With laughter and cheers, they just couldn't stop. The grand elephant spoke, with wisdom and might, "An organized circus, where everything's right."

The Donkey chimed in, with something to say. He stared at the crowd and stuttered away.

The crowd was divided, both sides had their say, The court jester chuckled, and juggled in dismay. The trapeze artists flipped, in confusion they hung, As the circus awaited, whose song would be sung.

But in the end, the grand elephant won, The applause was deafening, the circus begun. He promised a show, with excitement and cheer, For animals and humans, both far and near.

The lion bowed graciously, the monkey swung high, The old sleepy donkey just let out a sigh. For in this grand circus, with laughter and cheer, The animals rejoiced, as the election year cleared.

And so, my dear children, the tale is now done, Of the circus election, a victory hard-won. The grand elephant led, with wisdom and grace, A circus united, in a magical place.

Remember this story, as you dream in your bed, Of a circus where animals, both wild and well-fed, Elected their leader, with laughter and fun, In a magical circus, where dreams are begun.

Now close your eyes, let your dreams take flight, In a world filled with wonder, under the stars and stripes. For in every circus, a leader will stand, Guiding the way, with an elephant's command.

The End!

Thank You

Made in the USA
Las Vegas, NV
07 October 2024

96411240R00017